halloween
treats

KU-248-581

halloween treats
simply spooky recipes for ghoulish sweet treats

with recipes by Annie Rigg

photography by William Lingwood

LONDON • NEW YORK

To Ollie & Tom

Senior Designer Iona Hoyle
Commissioning Editor Céline Hughes
Production Gary Hayes
Art Director Leslie Harrington
Editorial Director Julia Charles

Prop Stylist Jo Harris
Indexer Hilary Bird

First published in 2012
by Ryland Peters & Small
20–21 Jockey's Fields
London WC1R 4BW
and
519 Broadway, 5th Floor
New York, NY 10012

www.rylandpeters.com

10 9 8 7 6 5 4 3 2 1

Text © Annie Rigg 2012, except pages 15 and 16
(Chloe Coker), 28 (Susannah Blake), and 32
(Hannah Miles).
Design and photographs © Ryland Peters & Small 2012

All photography by **William Lingwood**, except pages
10 and 11 (**Tara Fisher**); 14 and 15 inset (**Martin Norris**);
28, 30, 31, 39 background, 48 and 49 (**Kate Whitaker**);
29 (**Martin Brigdale**); 15 background, 32 and 33 (**Steve
Painter**); 38 and 39 inset (**Sandra Lane**).

Printed in China

The authors' moral rights have been asserted. All rights
reserved. No part of this publication may be
reproduced, stored in a retrieval system or transmitted in
any form or by any means, electronic, mechanical,
photocopying or otherwise, without the prior
permission of the publisher.

ISBN: 978-1-84975-252-7

A CIP record for this book is available from the British
Library.

Library of Congress Cataloging-in-Publication Data

Rigg, Annie.
 Halloween treats : simply spooky recipes for ghoulish
sweet treats / with recipes by Annie Rigg ;
photography by William Lingwood.
     p. cm.
 Includes index.
 ISBN 978-1-84975-252-7
 1. Halloween cooking. 2. Desserts. 1. Title.
 TX739.2.H34R54 2012
 641.5'68--dc23
                          2012013449

Notes

• All spoon measurements are level, unless otherwise
specified.

• Eggs used in this book are large, unless otherwise
specified.

• Butter used in this book is unsalted, unless otherwise
specified.

• Ovens should be preheated to the specified
temperatures. All ovens work slightly differently. We
recommend using an oven thermometer and suggest
you consult the maker's handbook for any special
instructions, particularly if you are cooking in a fan-
assisted/convection oven, as you will need to adjust
temperatures according to manufacturer's instructions.

Cake decorating suppliers
UK

Cakes Cookies & Crafts Shop, all manner of cake
decorating supplies including cupcake wrappers
www.cakescookiesandcraftsshop.co.uk

Jane Asher, for food colourings and sugarcraft supplies
www.jane-asher.co.uk

Squires, for food colourings (pastes and powders)
and various flavouring extracts
www.squires-shop.com

US

Kitchen Krafts, for cake decorating supplies
www.kitchenkrafts.com

Wilton, for decorating supplies for every occasion
www.wilton.com

contents

trick or treat?

Halloween has become a firm fixture on the party calendar and a Halloween party is simply not a party without a ghoulish spread of spooky treats and nibbles. Whether you are making party food for a houseful of little ghosts and goblins, or providing platters of snacks for the inevitable trick or treaters in your neighbourhood, you'll be in need of a good supply of home-baked goodies. In this book you'll find a selection of cupcakes, cookies and other treats that should be fearsome enough to scare even the spiders away.

Some of these recipes are fun for kids to help make as well as to eat – Brainball Clusters (page 61), Sugar Rats (page 53) and Severed Fingers (page 20) are easy for little hands to roll and shape. The cakes and cookies that require piping and a steady hand, such as the Mummified Cupcakes (page 35) and Glittery Ghosts (page 16) may need some supervision.

Most good online cake decorating suppliers now have special sections dedicated to all things Halloween – check out my suggestions on page 4. The range is eye-boggling, from cupcake picks, wrappers and paper cases, to sugar sprinkles in the traditional orange and green Halloween colours, and edible sugar eyes in varying sizes. Look for an eerie selection of cookie cutters in the shapes of witches' hats, cats, ghosts and spider's webs amongst others.

Of course there are also hundreds of related toys and candies to be found in party stores, supermarkets, candy stores and probably even in your cupboards at home! Dig out plastic spiders and rats, chocolate cookies such as Oreos and Bourbons to crush into 'earth' for lacing with disgusting gummy worms and caterpillars, licorice laces... even cotton wool to stretch and drape over furniture to resemble cobwebs.

As well as carving pumpkin jack-o'-lanterns to decorate your house and garden, you can also make mini pumpkins to scatter around your baked goodies. Simply tint storebought sugarpaste or marzipan using orange food colouring paste. Break off little nuggets and roll into pumpkins of assorted sizes. Use a cocktail stick or toothpick to mark ridges around the sides and make a stalk from green-coloured sugarpaste. Allow to dry for a couple of days, then arrange around your cupcakes and cookies for an extra special touch. If you just don't have the time to make these on top of your planned cakes or cookies, search for some ready-made ones – half the fun is in discovering the world of Halloween paraphernalia out there!

The fun starts now! Cast a few spells, dress up in your most scary costume and get baking!

cookies

GINGERBREAD DOUGH

2 tablespoons golden syrup/
light corn syrup

I egg yolk

200 g/1²/₃ cups plain/all-purpose
flour, plus extra for dusting

½ teaspoon baking powder

1½ teaspoons ground ginger

I teaspoon ground cinnamon

¼ teaspoon freshly grated nutmeg

a pinch of salt

100 g/7 tablespoons butter,
chilled and diced

75 g/⅓ cups light muscovado or light
brown (soft) sugar

TO DECORATE

500 g/3½ cups royal icing sugar/mix

green, black and orange food
colouring pastes

orange sanding sugar

round cookie cutter,
about 9 cm/3⅝ inches

baking sheets, lined with nonstick
baking parchment

disposable piping bags

MAKES 10–12

These cute cookies are even simpler to make than they seem because you can create them out of a plain round of dough – no fancy cookie cutters required.

jack-o'-lanterns

To make the gingerbread dough, beat together the syrup and egg yolk in a small bowl. Sift together the flour, baking powder, spices and salt into a mixing bowl and add the butter. Rub the butter in with your fingertips until the mixture starts to look like sand and there are no lumps left. Add the sugar and mix with your fingers again for 30 seconds to incorporate. Tip the mixture out onto a very lightly floured surface and knead gently to bring together into a smooth ball. Flatten into a disc, wrap in clingfilm/plastic wrap and refrigerate for 1–2 hours.

Preheat the oven to 170°C (325°F) Gas 3.

Lightly dust a clean, dry surface with flour and roll the dough to a thickness of 2–3 mm/⅛ inch. Use the cutter to stamp out as many cookies as possible, cutting each one as close as possible to the next. Arrange on the prepared baking sheets. Gather the scraps together, knead lightly, re-roll and stamp out more cookies until all the dough is used up. Bake in batches on the middle shelf of the preheated oven for 10–12 minutes or until firm and lightly browned at the edges. Allow to cool completely on the baking sheets.

To decorate, prepare the royal icing according to the pack instructions. Spoon 1–2 tablespoons into a small bowl and tint green using the food colouring paste. Tint another 3 tablespoons of the icing black. Cover and set aside. Tint the remaining icing a deep shade of orange. Spoon 3 tablespoons of it into a piping bag and pipe pumpkin-shaped outlines on each cookie. Use the green icing in the same way to make a stalk outline for each pumpkin. Allow to dry for at least 10 minutes. Flood the outlines with their corresponding colours. You can either do this with the piping bag again, or with a teaspoon or a tiny spatula. Make sure the icing evenly fills the outline. Allow to dry for 5 minutes before dusting the pumpkin shape with orange sanding sugar. Allow to dry for 15 minutes.

Pipe orange curved lines over each pumpkin. Allow to dry for 10–15 minutes. Fill another piping bag with the black icing and pipe eyes and mouths. Allow to dry completely before serving.

You might have made thumbprint cookies before – little discs of dough with a thumbprint indent filled with jam or similar – but have you ever made them like this?! If you prefer, you can buy ready-made sugar eyes from sugarcraft suppliers (see page 4).

eyeball cookies

100 g/6½ tablespoons butter, soft

50 g/3 tablespoons crunchy peanut butter

100 g/½ cup (caster) sugar

1 egg yolk

1 teaspoon pure vanilla extract

150 g/1 cup plus 2 tablespoons plain/all-purpose flour

a pinch of salt

TO DECORATE

50 g/2 oz. white ready-to-roll royal icing

blue, green and red food colouring pastes

300 g/10 oz. white chocolate, chopped

24 brown candy-coated chocolate drops

baking sheet, lined with nonstick baking parchment

MAKES ABOUT 24

Preheat the oven to 180°C (350°F) Gas 4.

Put the butter, peanut butter and sugar in a mixing bowl and cream until pale and light – 3–4 minutes. Add the egg yolk and vanilla extract and mix until combined. Tip the flour and salt into the bowl and mix again until smooth.

Pull off walnut-sized pieces of dough and roll into balls between your hands. Arrange on the prepared baking sheet. Press your finger into the top of each cookie to make an indent. Bake the cookies on the middle shelf of the preheated oven for about 12 minutes until golden and firm. Allow to cool on the baking sheet for 2–3 minutes before transferring to a wire rack until cold.

To decorate, divide the royal icing in half. Tint one portion bright blue by dipping a cocktail stick/toothpick into the colouring and applying it to the royal icing. Knead it in until the icing is brightly and evenly coloured. Repeat with the other icing using the green colouring paste. Divide the blue icing into 12 equal portions, roll into balls and flatten into discs. Repeat with the green icing. Cover them all with clingfilm/plastic wrap and set aside.

Melt the white chocolate in a heatproof bowl either in the microwave on a low setting or over a pan of barely simmering water. Do not let the base of the bowl touch the water. Stir until smooth, then allow to cool and thicken slightly.

Taking one cookie at a time, dip the top into the melted chocolate and place on a wire rack. Position either a blue or green icing disc in the dent in the middle of the cookie. Dip one side of a chocolate drop in the melted chocolate, then position on the icing disc.

Dip a cocktail stick/toothpick into the red food colouring paste and wiggle red, veiny lines across the white chocolate. Allow to set before serving.

These lovely hats are fun to make but they take a little sugarcrafting experience and patience. Make them when you've had some practice at decorating cookies otherwise they might look a bit too homemade!

witches' hats

I quantity gingerbread dough from Jack-o'-Lanterns (page II)

icing/confectioners' sugar, for dusting

300 g/IO oz. fondant or sugarpaste

purple, black and orange food colouring pastes

200 g/1½ cups royal icing sugar/mix

assorted witches' hat cutters

baking sheets, lined with nonstick baking parchment

disposable piping bags

MAKES 10–12

Make the gingerbread dough mixture from the Jack-o'-Lanterns recipe on page II.

Preheat the oven to I70°C (325°F) Gas 3.

Lightly dust a clean, dry surface with flour and roll the dough to a thickness of 2–3 mm/⅛ inch. Use the hat cutters to stamp out as many cookies as possible, cutting each one as close as possible to the next. Arrange on the prepared baking sheets. Gather the scraps together, knead lightly, re-roll and cut out more cookies until all the dough is used up. Bake in batches on the middle shelf of the preheated oven for IO–I2 minutes or until firm and lightly browned at the edges. Allow to cool completely on the baking sheets.

Put 50 g/2 oz. of the fondant or sugarpaste into one bowl and the rest in a second bowl. Tint the smaller portion purple by dipping a cocktail stick/toothpick into the colouring and applying it to the fondant. Knead it in until the fondant is evenly coloured. Repeat with the larger portion of fondant using the black colouring paste. Dust a surface with icing/confectioners' sugar and roll out the black fondant. Using the hat cutters, stamp out enough witches' hats to match the number of cookies and lay them over the cookies. Dab a little water on the cookies first, if necessary, to make the fondant stick.

Roll out some purple rolled fondant as thinly as possible. Cut some thin strips and stick them to the bottom of the hats as a trim.

Prepare the royal icing according to the pack instructions. Divide the icing in half and put each portion in its own bowl. Tint one bowl purple and the other orange using the food colouring pastes. Fill a piping bag with the orange icing and pipe stars, spiders and cobwebs on the hats, as well as studs and buckles on the purple trims.

These ghost cookies are ideal for taking to a friend's Halloween party as a sweet treat. You can make them in different colours, or keep them all white for a truly elegant group of ghosts. You can also bake them on lolly/popsicle sticks for an even cuter gift.

glittery ghosts

VANILLA COOKIE DOUGH

250 g/2½ cups plain/all-purpose flour

125 g/1¼ cups self-raising flour

a pinch of salt

250 g/2 sticks butter, soft

125 g/⅔ cup (caster) sugar

1 egg yolk

1 teaspoon pure vanilla extract

TO DECORATE

500 g/3½ cups royal icing sugar/mix

black food colouring paste

edible glitter

ghost cookie cutters

baking sheets, lined with nonstick baking parchment

disposable piping bags

MAKES ABOUT 12

To make the vanilla cookie dough, sift the flours and salt and set aside. Put the butter and sugar in a mixing bowl and cream until light and fluffy – 3–4 minutes. Beat in the egg yolk and vanilla extract until they are fully incorporated. Finally, add the sifted dry ingredients and mix until well incorporated and the mixture forms a dough. Do not overwork the dough. Flatten into a disc, wrap in clingfilm/plastic wrap and refrigerate for about 1–2 hours.

Preheat the oven to 200°C (400°F) Gas 6.

Lightly dust a clean, dry surface with flour and roll the dough to a thickness of 2–3 mm/⅛ inch. Use the cutter to stamp out as many cookies as possible. Arrange on the prepared baking sheets. Gather the scraps together, knead lightly, re-roll and stamp out more cookies until all the dough is used up. Bake in batches on the middle shelf of the preheated oven for 12–16 minutes or until golden at the edges. Allow to cool completely on the baking sheets.

To decorate, prepare the royal icing according to the pack instructions. Spoon about 1–2 tablespoons into a small bowl and tint black using the food colouring paste. Cover and set aside.

Fill a piping bag with the remaining, untinted icing. Carefully pipe a fine outline around the edge of each cookie. Allow to dry for at least 10 minutes before flooding the middle with more icing. You can either do this with the piping bag again, or with a teaspoon or a tiny spatula. Make sure the icing evenly fills the outline.

Lay the cookies on a sheet of baking parchment and sprinkle edible glitter evenly over them. Gently tip the cookies over to discard any excess glitter. By putting the cookies on baking parchment, you can collect any excess glitter and return it to its container.

Pipe white dots for eyes on each ghost, then fill another piping bag with the black royal icing and pipe black dots on top. Allow to dry completely before serving.

This is a rather gruesome take on sandwich cookies which will appeal more to older children. You don't need a special cutter to make the coffin shapes — just a steady hand or your own handmade paper template.

coffin sandwiches

225 g/15 tablespoons butter, soft

225 g/1 cup plus 2 tablespoons (caster) sugar

finely grated zest of ½ orange

1 egg, lightly beaten

½ teaspoon ground cinnamon

a pinch of salt

450 g/2¾ cups plain/all-purpose flour, plus extra for rolling out

FILLING

100 g/3½ oz. dark/semisweet chocolate, chopped

100 g/⅓ cup sweetened condensed milk

40 g/3 tablespoons butter, soft

TO DECORATE

100 g/3½ oz. dark/semisweet chocolate, chopped

100 g/3½ oz. white chocolate, chopped

baking sheets, lined with nonstick baking parchment

wide pastry brush

disposable piping bag

MAKES 8–10

Put the butter and sugar in a mixing bowl and cream until pale and light — 3–4 minutes. Add the orange zest, egg, cinnamon and salt and mix well. Gradually add the flour and mix until incorporated and smooth. Bring the dough together into a ball using your hands, flatten into a disc, wrap in clingfilm/plastic wrap and refrigerate for 2 hours or until firm.

Preheat the oven to 180°C (350°F) Gas 4.

Lightly dust a clean, dry surface with flour and roll the dough to a thickness of 2–3 mm/⅛ inch. Cut out as many rectangles as possible, 12 cm/5 inches long and 6 cm/2½ inches wide. Stack 4 rectangles on top of each other and trim off small triangles from the top corners and longer, thinner triangles from the bottom corners to make coffin shapes. Repeat until you've used up all the rectangles. Arrange the coffins on the prepared baking sheets in a single layer. Gather the scraps together, knead lightly, re-roll and cut out more cookies until all the dough is used up. Bake in batches on the middle shelf of the preheated oven for about 12 minutes or until lightly golden and firm to the touch. Allow to cool on the baking sheets for about 10 minutes before transferring to a wire rack until cold.

To make the filling, tip all the ingredients into a heatproof bowl and melt either over a saucepan of barely simmering water or in the microwave on a low setting. Stir until smooth, remove from the heat and allow to cool and thicken slightly.

Spread the filling over half the cookies and sandwich with another cookie.

To decorate, melt the dark/semisweet and white chocolates in separate bowls and stir until smooth. Spoon half the dark/semisweet melted chocolate into the white chocolate bowl and very gently stir until they are lightly swirled together. Using the pastry brush, paint the top cookie of each coffin with the marbled chocolate and allow to set.

Fill the piping bag with the remaining dark/semisweet melted chocolate and pipe a border around the top of each coffin, as well as initials if you like.

These cookies look super life-like and can be made more spooky if you paint some red food colouring around the base of each finger after baking. You could also put candy rings on the fingers and paint the fingernails in assorted (edible) colours.

severed fingers

125 g/1 stick butter, soft

25 g/2 tablespoons (caster) sugar

100 g/¾ cup icing/confectioners' sugar

2 egg yolks

1 teaspoon pure vanilla extract

275 g/2 cups plus 2 tablespoons plain/all-purpose flour

½ teaspoon baking powder

a pinch of salt

20 whole almonds, halved (this allows for breakages)

baking sheet, lined with nonstick baking parchment

MAKES ABOUT 24

Preheat the oven to 180°C (350°F) Gas 4.

Put the butter and both sugars in a mixing bowl and cream until pale and light – 3–4 minutes. Add the egg yolks and vanilla extract and mix until combined. Add the flour, baking powder and salt and mix again until smooth.

Break off small balls of dough and roll between your hands to make sausage shapes. Roll them no thicker than your own fingers. A good way to get a realistic finger effect is to splay your fingers when you roll your hand over the sausage of dough – you should get a bumpy outline to represent knuckles. Arrange on the prepared baking sheet. Press half an almond, flat side up, onto the end of each finger as a fingernail and use a round-bladed knife to mark ridges on each knuckle bone. Bake in batches on the middle shelf of the preheated oven for about 12 minutes until pale golden and firm. Allow to cool on the baking sheet for 2–3 minutes before transferring to a wire rack until cold.

Serve in individual boxes for an extra spooky surprise!

Here are some spiders with a glowing buttercream filling and licorice legs which are rather more cute than frightening! The granulated sugar coating is a clever touch that gives the cookies a slightly hairy appearance.

125 g/1 stick butter, soft

225 g/1 cup plus 2 tablespoons (caster) sugar

1 medium egg, lightly beaten

1 teaspoon pure vanilla extract

175 g/1⅓ cups plain/ all-purpose flour

50 g/⅓ cup unsweetened cocoa powder

½ teaspoon baking powder

½ teaspoon bicarbonate of/ baking soda

a pinch of salt

3 tablespoons granulated sugar

FILLING

100 g/6½ tablespoons butter, soft

150 g/1¼ cups icing/confectioners' sugar

1 teaspoon pure vanilla extract

green and orange food colouring pastes

TO DECORATE

48 green and orange candy-coated chocolate drops

black licorice strips

baking sheets, lined with nonstick baking parchment

disposable piping bag

MAKES ABOUT 24

spider cookies

Preheat the oven to 180°C (350°F) Gas 4.

Put the butter and (caster) sugar in a mixing bowl and cream until pale and light – 3–4 minutes. Add the egg and vanilla extract and mix until combined.

Sift the flour, cocoa powder, baking powder, bicarbonate of/baking soda and salt into the mixing bowl and mix again until thoroughly combined and the cookie dough is smooth.

Pull off pieces of dough about the size of large marbles and roll into balls between your hands. Press the top of each cookie into the granulated sugar and arrange on the prepared baking sheets, then slightly flatten each one with your fingers. Bake on the middle shelf of the preheated oven for no more than 12 minutes – do not allow to over-bake otherwise they will become bitter. Allow to cool on the baking sheets while you prepare the filling.

To make the filling, put the butter, sugar and vanilla extract in a mixing bowl and cream until pale and light – 3–4 minutes. Remove 2 tablespoons of this buttercream and set aside. Divide the remaining buttercream in half and tint one portion green and one portion orange using the food colouring pastes.

Spread orange buttercream over the underside of 12 of the cookies and the green buttercream over the underside of another 12. Top with the remaining cookies.

To decorate, spoon the untinted buttercream into the disposable piping bag and pipe 2 eyes on top of each spider. Press the green and orange chocolate drops onto the buttercream eyes.

Cut the licorice strips into small spider-leg lengths – you will need 8 for each cookie – and push into the sides of each spider to serve.

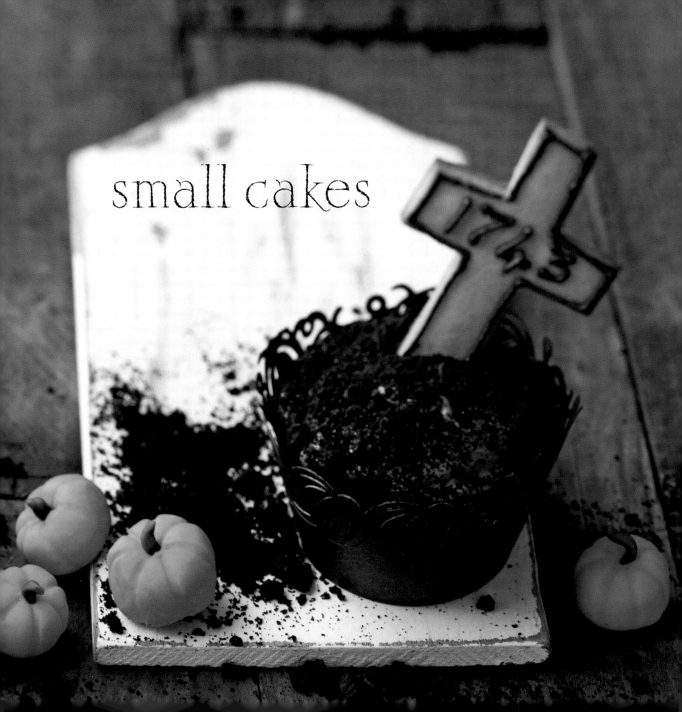

small cakes

These cupcakes are a spooky version of much loved 'hi-hat' cupcakes with their mound of marshmallowy frosting. You can make the cakes a day in advance but the frosting should be made on the day of serving.

ghostly cupcakes

RED VELVET CAKE

175 g/1½ sticks butter, soft

250 g/1¼ cups (caster) sugar

2 eggs, lightly beaten

1 teaspoon pure vanilla extract

½ teaspoon red food colouring paste

125 ml/½ cup buttermilk, at room temperature

175 g/1⅓ cups plain/all-purpose flour

2 tablespoons unsweetened cocoa powder

a pinch of salt

1 teaspoon bicarbonate of/ baking soda

1 teaspoon white vinegar

black food colouring paste

edible glitter

MARSHMALLOW FROSTING

250 g/1¼ cups caster/superfine sugar

4 egg whites

½ teaspoon pure vanilla extract

a pinch of salt

12-hole muffin pan, lined with white paper cases

sugar thermometer

large piping bag, fitted with a plain 1-cm/⅜-inch nozzle

MAKES 12

Preheat the oven to 180°C (350°F) Gas 4.

Put the butter and sugar in a mixing bowl and cream until pale and light – 3–4 minutes. Gradually add the eggs and vanilla extract, mixing well between each addition and scraping down the sides of the bowl with a rubber spatula from time to time.

Mix the red food colouring with the buttermilk until evenly coloured. In another bowl, sift together the flour, cocoa powder and salt. Add the sifted dry ingredients to the cake mixture in alternate batches with the red buttermilk and mix until smooth.

In a small bowl, mix together the bicarbonate of/baking soda and vinegar, then quickly add to the cake mixture and mix until thoroughly incorporated.

Divide the mixture between the paper cases and bake on the middle shelf of the preheated oven for about 20 minutes or until well risen and a skewer inserted into the middle of the cakes comes out clean. Allow to cool in the muffin pan for 3 minutes before transferring to a wire rack until cold.

To make the marshmallow frosting, put the sugar, egg whites, vanilla extract and salt in a medium heatproof bowl set over a pan of simmering water. Whisk slowly with a balloon whisk until the sugar has dissolved, the mixture starts to thicken and turn white and it reaches 60°C/140°F on a sugar thermometer – about 4 minutes. Remove from the heat and whisk with an electric whisk on medium speed for another 3 minutes or until cold, very thick and glossy white.

Immediately spoon the frosting into the piping bag and pipe the meringue into a swirly cone shape on top of each cupcake.

Tint 3 teaspoons of the marshmallow frosting black using the food colouring paste and pipe eyes on the ghosts.

Finally, sprinkle edible glitter over the ghosts. Boo!

Sweet, spicy pumpkin cakes topped with these spooky chocolate cobwebs are definitely a treat rather than a trick. You can leave the topping to set completely if you like, but it's so much better when it's still soft.

cobweb cupcakes

115 g/½ cup light brown (soft) sugar

125 ml/½ cup sunflower oil

2 medium eggs

115 g/1 cup grated pumpkin or butternut squash flesh

grated zest of 1 unwaxed lemon

115 g/1 cup self-raising flour

1 teaspoon baking powder

1 teaspoon ground cinnamon

TO DECORATE

150 g/5 oz. white chocolate, chopped

25 g/1 oz. dark/bittersweet chocolate, chopped

12-hole muffin pan, lined with foil cases

disposable piping bag

MAKES 12

Preheat the oven to 180°C (350°F) Gas 4.

Put the sugar in a bowl and break up with the back of a fork, then beat in the oil and eggs. Fold in the grated pumpkin and lemon zest. In another bowl, sift together the flour, baking powder and cinnamon. Add the sifted dry ingredients to the cake mixture and fold in.

Divide the mixture between the foil cases and bake on the middle shelf of the preheated oven for about 18 minutes or until risen and a skewer inserted into the middle of the cakes comes out clean. Transfer to a wire rack until cold.

To decorate, melt the dark/semisweet and white chocolates in separate heatproof bowls either in the microwave on a low setting or over a pan of barely simmering water. Do not let the base of the bowl touch the water. Stir until smooth, then allow to cool for about 5 minutes. Spoon the white chocolate over the cakes.

Spoon the dark/bittersweet chocolate into the piping bag and pipe a dot of chocolate in the middle of each cake, then pipe three concentric circles around the dot.

Using a skewer, draw a line from the central dot to the outside edge of the cake and repeat about eight times all the way round to create a spider's web pattern. Serve while the chocolate is still slightly soft and gooey.

Make a whole gathering of these little carved pumpkin-shaped cakes and scatter them around the room for your Halloween party. Look for orange, green or black paper cases and Halloween sprinkles to decorate the serving dish.

jack-o'-lantern cupcakes

1 quantity vanilla cake mixture from Mummified Cupcakes (page 35)

1 quantity meringue buttercream from Mummified Cupcakes (page 35)

black food colouring paste

orange food colouring paste

orange sanding sugar or nonpareils

green jelly beans or fruity pastilles, for the stalks

Halloween sprinkles (optional), to decorate the serving dish

12-hole muffin pan, lined with white paper cases

small piping bag, fitted with a small star nozzle/tip

MAKES 12–16

Preheat the oven to 180°C (350°F) Gas 4.

Make and bake the vanilla cake cupcakes from the Mummified Cupcakes recipe on page 35.

Make the meringue buttercream from the Mummified Cupcakes recipe on page 35. Put in a bowl, take out 6 tablespoons and transfer to a separate bowl. Tint this quantity black using the food colouring paste. Colour the remaining, large bowl of buttercream orange.

Spread the orange buttercream over the cold cupcakes, spreading evenly with a palette knife. Using the blunt end of a knife or a wooden skewer, make indents in the buttercream to resemble ridges in the pumpkins. Scatter orange sanding sugar or nonpareils over the buttercream until evenly coated.

Fill the piping bag with the black buttercream. Pipe eyes, a nose and a mouth onto the orange frosting to make jack-o'-lantern faces. Lay the cupcakes on their side and stick one green jelly bean into the top of each cupcake to make the stalks.

Scatter the serving dish with Halloween sugar sprinkles, if using, and arrange the cupcakes on top to serve.

125 g/1 stick butter or vegetable shortening, soft

200 g/1 cup dark brown (soft) sugar

1 egg

140 g/²⁄₃ cup canned pumpkin purée

340 g/2²⁄₃ cups self-raising flour

2 teaspoons ground cinnamon

1 teaspoon ground mixed spice/ apple pie spice

1 teaspoon ground ginger

1 teaspoon baking powder

½ teaspoon salt

250 ml/1 cup plain yogurt

100 ml/⅓ cup hot (not boiling) water

CREAM CHEESE FILLING

200 g/7 oz. cream cheese

125 g/1 stick butter, soft

400 g/3¼ cups icing/ confectioners' sugar

TO DECORATE

200 g/1²⁄₃ cups, plus 3 big tablespoons fondant icing/ confectioners' sugar

juice of 1 small orange

green, orange and red food colouring pastes

2 chocolate sticks

two 12-hole whoopie pie pans, greased

3 piping bags, fitted with a large star nozzle/tip, a small plain nozzle/tip, and a leaf nozzle/tip

MAKES 12

Whoopie pies are so cute and delicious. For the best, neatest results, buy a whoopie pie pan. Decorated as cute pumpkins, these buttery, spiced pumpkin pies make a perfect Halloween treat for kids and adults alike!

pumpkin pies

Preheat the oven to 180°C (350°F) Gas 4.

Put the butter and brown sugar in a mixing bowl and cream for 2–3 minutes using an electric whisk, until light and creamy. Add the egg and pumpkin purée and mix again. Sift the flour, cinnamon, mixed/apple pie spice, ginger and baking powder into the bowl and add the salt and yogurt. Whisk until everything is incorporated. Add the hot water and whisk into the mixture.

Put a large spoonful of mixture into each hole in the prepared pie pans. Allow to stand for 10 minutes, then bake in the preheated oven for 10–12 minutes. Remove the pies from the oven and allow to cool slightly before turning out onto a wire rack until cold.

To make the cream cheese filling, whisk together the cream cheese, butter and icing/ confectioners' sugar until light and creamy. Remove 4 tablespoons of the mixture, mix in a drop of green food colouring, cover and set aside. Spoon the remaining filling into a piping bag fitted with the large star nozzle/tip and pipe a generous swirl of filling onto 12 of the pie halves. Set aside.

To decorate, first make an orange glacé icing. Mix together the 200 g/1²⁄₃ cups icing/ confectioners' sugar, orange juice and a few dots of orange food colouring until you have smooth, glossy icing. Cover the remaining pie halves with the icing using a round-bladed knife and allow to set. When the icing has set, mix the 3 tablespoons of icing/confectioners' sugar with 1–2 teaspoons cold water and a few dots of orange and red food colouring to make a thick, darker orange icing. Spoon the icing into a piping bag fitted with a small plain nozzle/tip and pipe 5 lines from the middle of each pie (to resemble the ridges on a pumpkin). Spoon the green cream cheese filling into a clean piping bag fitted with a leaf nozzle and pipe green leaves and a curly stem on top of each pie, as shown. Cut each chocolate stick into 6 pieces and stick in the middle to look like stalks.

Top the cream cheese filling-topped pie halves with the decorated pie halves and your whoopie pies are ready to enjoy.

Look for edible sugar eyes from online sugarcraft suppliers (see page 4) but if you can't find them you could just as easily use coloured candy-coated chocolate drops or even pipe little black eyes using black writing icing.

mummified cupcakes

24 edible sugar eyes

VANILLA CAKE

225 g/15 tablespoons butter, soft

225 g/1 cup plus 2 tablespoons (caster) sugar

4 eggs, lightly beaten

1 teaspoon pure vanilla extract

225 g/1¾ cups self-raising flour

2 tablespoons milk

MERINGUE BUTTERCREAM

200 g/1 cup caster/superfine sugar

3 egg whites

250 g/2 sticks butter, soft and diced

1 teaspoon pure vanilla extract

12-hole muffin pan, lined with white paper cases

sugar thermometer

piping bag, fitted with a 1-cm/³⁄₈-inch flat-sided nozzle/tip

MAKES 12

Preheat the oven to 180°C (350°F) Gas 4.

Put the butter and sugar in a mixing bowl and cream until pale and light – about 3–4 minutes. Gradually add the eggs and vanilla extract, mixing well between each addition and scraping down the sides of the bowl with a rubber spatula from time to time.

Sift the flour into the cake mixture and mix until thoroughly combined. Add the milk and mix until smooth.

Divide the mixture between the paper cases and bake on the middle shelf of the preheated oven for about 20–25 minutes or until golden, well risen and a skewer inserted into the middle of the cakes comes out clean. Allow to cool in the muffin pan for 3 minutes before transferring to a wire rack until cold.

To make the meringue buttercream, put the sugar and egg whites in a heatproof bowl set over a pan of simmering water. Whisk slowly with a balloon whisk until the sugar has dissolved, the mixture starts to thicken and turn white and it reaches 60°C/140°F on a sugar thermometer – about 4 minutes. Remove from the heat and whisk with an electric whisk on medium speed for another 3 minutes or until cold, very thick and glossy white. Gradually add the diced butter, beating constantly until the butter has been incorporated and the frosting is smooth. Fold in the vanilla extract.

Immediately spoon the frosting into the piping bag and pipe bands across the cupcakes from side to side, allowing some bands to overlap slightly. Press 2 sugar eyes into the frosting on each mummified cupcake.

These cookie headstones can be made the day before you plan to serve the cupcakes. Look for cupcake wrappers with a Halloween design – pumpkins or picket fences and haunted houses would all be perfect.

graveyard cupcakes

1 quantity red velvet mixture from Ghostly Cupcakes (page 27)

½ quantity cinnamon cookie dough from Coffin Sandwiches (page 19)

TO DECORATE

150 g/1 cup royal icing sugar/mix

black food colouring paste

150 g/5 oz. dark/semisweet chocolate

1 quantity meringue buttercream from Mummified Cupcakes (page 35) but follow method here

6 Oreo or Bourbon cookies

mini sugarpaste or marzipan pumpkins, to decorate (see page 7)

12-hole muffin pan, lined with 12 black/brown cupcake cases

card templates in the shape of cross headstones

baking sheet, lined with nonstick baking parchment

disposable piping bag

12 black cupcake wrappers

MAKES 12

Make and bake the red velvet cupcakes from the Ghostly Cupcakes recipe on page 27.

Prepare the cinnamon cookie dough from the Coffin Sandwiches recipe on page 19. When it has chilled for 2 hours, lightly dust a clean, dry surface with flour and roll the dough to a thickness of 2–3 mm/⅛ inch. Lay your cross template on the dough and carefully cut around it with a small, sharp knife. Cut out as many crosses as there are cupcakes, plus a couple extra to allow for breakages. Arrange on the prepared baking sheet. Bake on the middle shelf of the preheated oven for 10–12 minutes or until firm and lightly browned at the edges. Allow to cool completely on the baking sheets.

To decorate, prepare the royal icing according to the pack instructions to make a thick writing icing and tint it black using the food colouring paste. Spoon into the piping bag and pipe an outline around each headstone. Pipe dates or names on the headstones too, if you like.

Melt the dark/semisweet chocolate in a bowl and stir until smooth. Allow to cool until almost cold. Meanwhile, prepare the meringue buttercream from the Mummified Cupcakes recipe on page 35. Add the cooled, melted chocolate once all the butter has been incorporated.

Crush the Oreo or Bourbon cookies finely in a food processor or put them in a freezer bag, seal and crush with a rolling pin. They should become fine enough to resemble earth.

Cover the top of each cupcake with the chocolate meringue buttercream, scatter the crushed cookies over them and push the headstone into one side. Carefully wrap each cupcake in a black cupcake wrapper. Decorate the scene with mini sugarpaste or marzipan pumpkins to serve.

The cupcakes and chocolate-coated cones for these hats can be prepared in advance and assembled on the day of your party. Try to find a good selection of ghoulish treats and candies to fill the cones with.

wizards' hats cakes

1 quantity red velvet mixture from Ghostly Cupcakes (page 27)

300 g/10 oz. dark/semisweet chocolate, chopped

18–20 ice cream cones

edible silver balls

TO DECORATE

150 g/5 oz. dark/semisweet chocolate, chopped

1 quantity meringue buttercream from Mummified Cupcakes (page 35) but follow method here

assorted sprinkles

assorted candies

12-hole muffin pans, lined with foil cases

MAKES 12

Make and bake the red velvet cupcakes from the Ghostly Cupcakes recipe on page 27.

Melt the 300 g/10 oz. dark/semisweet chocolate in a heatproof bowl either in the microwave on a low setting or over a pan of barely simmering water. Do not let the base of the bowl touch the water. Stir until smooth. Hold an ice cream cone over the bowl of chocolate and pour the melted chocolate over with a spoon until the cone is evenly coated, allowing any excess chocolate to drip back into the bowl. Scatter with edible silver balls, then stand the hats upright on a tray and allow to set.

To decorate, melt the 150 g/5 oz. dark/semisweet chocolate in a bowl as above. Allow to cool until almost cold. Meanwhile, prepare the meringue buttercream from the Mummified Cupcakes recipe on page 35. Add the cooled, melted chocolate once all the butter has been incorporated.

Cover the top of each cupcake with a swirl of chocolate meringue buttercream and scatter assorted sprinkles over the top. Fill the chocolate-coated ice cream cones with candies and stick one on top of each cupcake.

big cakes

CHOCOLATE CAKE

200 g/13 tablespoons butter, soft

325 g/1²/₃ cups (caster) sugar

4 eggs, lightly beaten

I teaspoon pure vanilla extract

125 g/4 oz. dark/semisweet chocolate

300 g/2¹/₃ cups plain/
all-purpose flour

2 rounded tablespoons unsweetened
cocoa powder

I teaspoon baking powder

2 teaspoons bicarbonate of/
baking soda

a pinch of salt

225 ml/1 cup sour cream,
at room temperature

175 ml/²/₃ cup boiling water

CHOCOLATE FUDGE FROSTING

225 g/8 oz. dark/semisweet
chocolate, chopped

150 g/10 tablespoons butter

125 ml/¹/₂ cup whole milk

225 g/2 cups icing/confectioners'
sugar

I teaspoon pure vanilla extract

TO FINISH

6 tablespoons apricot jam

250 ml/1 cup double/heavy cream

green food colouring paste

assorted candies

chocolate-coated finger cookies

*2 x 18-cm/7-inch and 1 x 20-cm/
8-inch cake pans, greased and
baselined with greased
baking parchment*

SERVES 14–16

Fill this chocolate cauldron cake with a selection of spooky candies and maybe a dusting of popping candy for a little extra whizz in your witches' brew. Cast a few magic spells, chuck in a couple of toads, newts and mice, and shazam!

cauldron cake

Preheat the oven to 180°C (350°F) Gas 4.

To make the chocolate cake, put the butter and sugar in a mixing bowl and cream until pale and light – 3–4 minutes. Gradually add the eggs and vanilla extract, mixing well between each addition and scraping down the sides of the bowl with a rubber spatula from time to time. Melt the dark/semisweet chocolate in a bowl and stir until smooth. Add the melted chocolate to the cake mixture and mix until combined.

In another bowl, sift together the flour, cocoa powder, baking powder, bicarbonate of/ baking soda and salt. Add one third of the sifted dry ingredients to the cake mixture and mix on low speed until combined, then add one-third of the sour cream. Repeat this process until you have used up all the dry ingredients and sour cream. Add the boiling water and mix until silky smooth. Divide the mixture between the prepared cake pans and bake on the middle shelf of the preheated oven for about 25 minutes or until well risen and a skewer inserted into the middle of the cakes comes out clean. Allow to cool in the cake pan for 3 minutes before transferring to a wire rack until cold.

To make the chocolate fudge frosting, melt the chocolate and butter together until smooth and allow to cool. In another bowl, whisk together the milk, sugar and vanilla extract. Stir in the cooled chocolate mixture and beat until smooth and thickened.

Place one of the smaller cakes on a serving dish, spread chocolate fudge frosting over the top and lay the larger cake on top. Spread frosting over the top. Using a 10-cm/ 4-inch round cookie cutter (or cutting around a plate/bowl of that size) stamp out and discard a disc from the middle of the last cake. Place the resulting cake ring on top of the stack of cakes and press gently together. Using a sharp knife, shave off the sides of the cakes so that the edges become rounded and cauldron-shaped.

To finish, brush the whole cake with warmed, strained apricot jam and refrigerate for 15 minutes.

Cover the whole cake with the remaining frosting, spreading the sides as smoothly as possible. Whip the cream until soft peaks form, then gently fold in some green food colouring paste. Spoon into the top of the cake and scatter the candies on top. Arrange the chocolate fingers around the bottom of the cake as firewood.

Look online for simple bat shapes to use as templates for the topping for this cake. I recommend using ready-made black sugarpaste to make the shapes, as it can be tricky to achieve a good, solid black colour with food colouring paste.

bat cake

VANILLA BUTTERMILK CAKE

225 g/2 sticks butter, soft

350 g/1¾ cups (caster) sugar

4 eggs, lightly beaten

1 teaspoon pure vanilla extract

350 g/2⅔ cups plain/
all-purpose flour

3 teaspoons baking powder

1 teaspoon bicarbonate of/
baking soda

a pinch of salt

250 ml/1 cup buttermilk

TO DECORATE

1 quantity meringue buttercream from
Mummified Cupcakes (page 35)

500 g/1 lb. white ready-to-roll
royal icing

orange food colouring paste

250 g/8 oz. black sugarpaste or
ready-to-roll icing

icing/confectioners' sugar,
for dusting

2 x 23-cm/9-inch cake pans,
greased and baselined with
greased baking parchment

card templates in the shapes of
bats: one roughly 23 cm/9 inches
wide and one roughly
10 cm/4 inches wide

SERVES 12–14

To make the vanilla buttermilk cake, preheat the oven to 180°C (350°F) Gas 4.

Put the butter and sugar in a mixing bowl and cream until pale and light – about 3–4 minutes. Gradually add the eggs and vanilla extract, mixing well between each addition and scraping down the sides of the bowl with a rubber spatula from time to time.

In another bowl, sift together the flour, baking powder, bicarbonate of/baking soda and salt. Add the sifted dry ingredients to the cake mixture alternately with the buttermilk. Mix until smooth. Divide the mixture evenly between the prepared cake pans. Spread level and bake on the middle shelf of the preheated oven for about 25 minutes or until well risen and a skewer inserted into the middle of the cakes comes out clean. Allow to cool in the cake pans for 3 minutes before transferring to a wire rack until cold.

To decorate, make the meringue buttercream from the Mummified Cupcakes recipe on page 35.

If the baked cakes are very domed, level them off with a large, serrated knife. Place one cake on a serving dish and spread meringue buttercream over the top. Lay the second cake on top and press gently together. Cover the whole cake with the remaining buttercream, spreading it as smoothly as possible. Refrigerate for 20 minutes.

Reserve a tiny amount of white icing for the bat eyes and set aside. Tint the remainder a spooky shade of orange using the food colouring paste. Lightly dust the work surface with icing/confectioners' sugar and roll out the icing into a disc larger enough to completely cover the top and side of the frosted cake. Roll the icing around the rolling pin, then carefully unroll it over the cake, neatly covering the top and side. Smooth the icing with your hands and trim off any excess with a knife.

Roll out the black icing into a disc about 25 cm/10 inches in diameter. With a small, sharp knife, cut out one large bat and 2 small ones using the templates. Brush a little water over the top of the cake and carefully position the bats on top. Roll tiny lumps of the reserved white icing into balls and stick in place with water for the bats' eyes.

These little ghost meringues can be made 1–2 days before you plan to serve this cake, as they will keep well in an airtight box. It's funny how each meringue seems to have a different expression by simply painting on some eyes!

ghoulish cake

1 quantity meringues from Meringue Bones (page 62) but follow method here

1 quantity chocolate cake from Cauldron Cake (page 43)

TO DECORATE

1 quantity meringue buttercream from Mummified Cupcakes (page 35)

100 g/3 $\frac{1}{2}$ oz. dark/semisweet chocolate, finely chopped

125 ml/ $\frac{1}{2}$ cup double/heavy cream

1 tablespoon light brown (soft) sugar

25 g/2 tablespoons butter

black writing icing

piping bag, fitted with a 1-cm/$\frac{3}{8}$-inch plain nozzle/tip

baking sheet, lined with baking parchment

2 x 23-cm/9-inch cake pans, greased and baselined with greased baking parchment

SERVES 12

Make the meringue ghosts the day before you make the cake. Preheat the oven to 110°C (225°F) Gas ¼.

Prepare the meringue mixture from the Meringue Bones recipe on page 62. Spoon into the piping bag and pipe into slightly wobbly cone shapes on the prepared baking sheet. Bake on the middle shelf of the preheated oven for 1 hour or until crisp. Turn the oven off and leave the ghosts to cool inside.

When you are ready to make the cake, preheat the oven to 180°C (350°F) Gas 4.

Make the chocolate cake mixture from the Cauldron Cake recipe on page 43 and divide evenly between the prepared cake pans. Bake on the middle shelf of the preheated oven for 20–25 minutes or until well risen and a skewer inserted into the middle of the cakes comes out clean. Allow to cool in the cake pans for 3 minutes before transferring to a wire rack until cold.

To decorate, make the meringue buttercream from the Mummified Cupcakes recipe on page 35. If the baked cakes are very domed, level them off with a large, serrated knife. Place one cake on a serving dish and spread meringue buttercream over the top. Lay the second cake on top and press gently together. Cover the whole cake with the remaining buttercream, spreading it as smoothly as possible. Refrigerate for 20 minutes.

Put the chocolate in a heatproof bowl. Heat the cream and sugar in a small pan until boiling. Pour over the chocolate and allow to melt. Add the butter and stir until smooth. Allow to cool and thicken slightly before spreading over the top of the cake and allowing to dribble over the sides. Use the black writing icing to give each of the ghosts eyes and arrange on top of the cake just before serving.

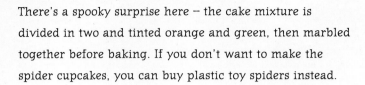

I quantity vanilla buttermilk
cake from Bat Cake
(page 44)

orange, green and black
food colouring pastes

TO DECORATE

I quantity meringue
buttercream from Mummified
Cupcakes (page 35)

2 tablespoons black sprinkles
or sanding sugar

black licorice strips

green and/or orange
sanding sugar

mini orange or yellow candy-
coated chocolate drops

250 g/2 cups royal icing
sugar/mix

*two 20-cm/8-inch round
cake pans, greased and
baselined with greased
baking parchment*

*15-cm/6-inch round
cake pan, greased and
baselined with greased
baking parchment*

*muffin pan, lined with
2–3 cupcake cases*

disposable piping bag

SERVES 8–10

There's a spooky surprise here – the cake mixture is divided in two and tinted orange and green, then marbled together before baking. If you don't want to make the spider cupcakes, you can buy plastic toy spiders instead.

creepy cake

Preheat the oven to 180°C (350°F) Gas 4.

Prepare the vanilla buttermilk cake mixture from the Bat Cake recipe on page 44. Divide the mixture between 2 bowls, and using the food colouring pastes, tint one bowl orange and the other green. Drop alternate spoonfuls of the 2 mixtures into the prepared cake pans, filling them halfway up. Fill the cupcake cases with alternate tablespoons of the cake mixtures, too. Tap the cake pans sharply on a surface to level the mixture and drag a round-bladed knife through the 2 mixtures to create a marbled effect. Tap the cake on the surface again. Repeat this process with the cupcakes in the muffin pan.

Bake everything on the middle shelves of the preheated oven for about 20–35 minutes, depending on their size, until a skewer inserted into the middle comes out clean. Let cool in the pans for 3–4 minutes before transferring to a wire rack until cold.

To decorate, make the meringue buttercream from the Mummified Cupcakes recipe on page 35. Tint 4 tablespoons black using the food colouring paste. If the baked cakes are very domed, level them off with a large, serrated knife. Place one of the larger cakes on a serving dish and spread some untinted buttercream over it. Top with the second larger cake and gently press the cakes together. Spread a thin layer of untinted buttercream over the top and side of the cake, then refrigerate for 10 minutes. Cover the cake with another thin layer of untinted buttercream. Repeat this process with the smaller cake.

Peel the cases off the cupcakes and slice the cupcakes in half horizontally. Cover with the black buttercream and scatter the black sprinkles or sanding sugar evenly over them to coat. Press short lengths of the licorice into the sides of the cupcakes as spider's legs and give each spider 2 orange or yellow eyes with the candy-coated chocolate drops.

Place the smaller cake on top of the larger cake. Sprinkle sanding sugar over the cake. Prepare the royal icing according to the pack instructions to make a thick writing icing and tint it black. Spoon into the piping bag and pipe spider's webs all over the cake. Arrange the spiders around the cake.

Here is my spooky spin on the sugar mice that are often made and served at Christmas time. Arrange the rats all around the party table, coming out of paper bags and from under bowls for extra spookiness.

sugar rats

150 g/²/₃ cup sweetened condensed milk

200 g/1¹/₂ cups icing/confectioners' sugar, plus 4 tablespoons

200 g/1¹/₃ cups desiccated coconut

black food colouring paste

red sour licorice laces

pink food colouring paste

disposable piping bags

MAKES 12

Tip the condensed milk, 200 g/1¹/₂ cups icing/confectioners' sugar and the desiccated coconut into a mixing bowl and stir with a wooden spoon until the mixture starts to come together. You may find it easier to use your hands to incorporate the last of the sugar as the mixture becomes quite stiff. Add black food colouring paste a little at a time and continue to mix until smooth and evenly coloured.

Break off walnut-size pieces of mixture and roll into a cone shape in your hands. Pinch 2 little ears on the narrow end of each cone and squeeze the point into a nose shape.

Using a skewer, poke a hole into the fat end of each rat and push a length of red licorice in to make a tail.

Allow the rats to dry on a sheet of baking parchment for at least 2 hours.

Make up a small amount of royal icing by mixing the remaining icing/confectioners' sugar with a little water until smooth but stiff enough to pipe. Transfer 1 tablespoon of the icing to another bowl and tint pink using the food colouring paste. Tint another 2 teaspoons of the icing black and leave the remainder white.

Spoon each colour of icing into a separate piping bag. Pipe 2 white eyes and one pink nose on each rat and allow the icing to dry for 5 minutes. Pipe a small black dot on each eye and allow to dry completely before serving.

Make these jellies on the morning of the party (rather than the day before) and fill with a gruesome combination of confectionery spiders, worms and teeth. These look particularly good in jars, so dig them out if you have some, otherwise glasses are just fine.

swampy jellies

6 gelatin leaves

750 ml/3 cups lime (or other green-coloured) cordial drink, made according to taste

(caster) sugar, to taste

green food colouring paste

gummy worms and other creepy Halloween candy

6–8 glasses or glass jars

SERVES 6–8

Soak the gelatin leaves in a dish of cold water for 3 minutes or until softened.

Heat half the cordial drink in a saucepan until just below boiling point, then remove from the heat. Drain the gelatin leaves, squeeze out any excess water, add to the hot juice and stir until melted. Add the remaining cordial drink and sugar, to taste. Using a cocktail stick/toothpick, add a little green food colouring paste to make the jelly a truly slimey colour.

Allow the jelly to cool until it just starts to thicken and is slightly lumpy. Pour the jelly into the glasses or glass jars and leave until almost set. Push the gummy worms and other creepy Halloween candy into the jelly and refrigerate until completely set. Serve with a few extra creepy crawlies on the side.

These doughnuts are baked rather than fried and are no
less delicious for it. They are filled with blood-red jam, but
they could have a chocolate or toffee filling if you prefer
and a dusting of edible glitter for a final flourish.

blood-filled doughnuts

175 ml/²⁄₃ cup whole milk

75 g/¹⁄₃ cup (caster) sugar

10 g/1 tablespoon active dried yeast

400 g/3¹⁄₄ cups strong white bread flour, plus extra for dusting

40 g/4 tablespoons unsweetened cocoa powder

¹⁄₂ teaspoon salt

2 medium eggs, lightly beaten

75 g/5 tablespoons butter, soft

TO FINISH

4–5 tablespoons seedless strawberry jam

25 g/2 tablespoons butter, melted

6 tablespoons caster/superfine sugar

5-cm/2-inch round cutter

2 baking sheets covered with baking parchment

disposable piping bag

MAKES ABOUT 20

Heat the milk in a small saucepan until just below boiling point. Remove from the heat and allow to cool until lukewarm. Add 1 teaspoon of the sugar and all the yeast and whisk to combine. Leave in a warm place for 5 minutes, or until the yeast has formed a thick foam on top of the milk.

Mix the flour, cocoa powder, salt and the remaining sugar in a large bowl. Make a well in the middle and add the eggs, butter and yeasty milk mixture. Mix with a wooden spoon until it comes together into a rough dough.
Tip out onto a lightly floured work surface and knead for about 5 minutes until it becomes silky smooth and elastic. Shape into a ball, place in a large bowl, cover with clingfilm/plastic wrap and leave in a warm place for about 1¹⁄₂ hours or until doubled in size.

When the dough has doubled in size, lightly dust a clean, dry surface with flour, tip the dough out onto it and knead again for 30 seconds. Roll it out to a thickness of about 1 cm/¹⁄₂ inch. Use the cutter to stamp out as many discs as possible, cutting each one as close as possible to the next. Arrange on the prepared baking sheets, cover loosely with oiled clingfilm/plastic wrap and leave in a warm place for another 40 minutes or until doubled in size.

Preheat the oven to 180°C (350°F) Gas 4.

Bake the doughnuts, one sheet at a time, on the middle shelf of the preheated oven for about 10–12 minutes. Allow to cool for 15 minutes.

To finish, spoon the jam into the piping bag. Using a skewer, poke a hole into the side of each doughnut and fill with about a teaspoon of jam. Brush each doughnut with melted butter and roll in the sugar to coat.

Look for small, preferably red-skinned apples and red lolly/
popsicle sticks for these fun and popular toffee/candy apples.
When you come to buy the ingredients for this recipe, why not get
some extra apples and at your party, fill a large tub with water,
tip in the apples and play bobbing for apples.

toffee apples

8 small apples, eg Cox's, Jazz,
Macoun or Pink Lady

300 g/1½ cups (caster) sugar

2 tablespoons golden syrup or
light corn syrup

juice of ½ lemon

TO DECORATE

assorted orange, green and black
sprinkles, for dipping

8 lolly/popsicle sticks or
wooden skewers

MAKES 8

Wash and thoroughly dry each apple. Carefully push a lolly/popsicle stick
or wooden skewer into the stalk end of each apple.

Put the sugar, syrup and 150 ml/⅔ cup water in a heavy-based saucepan
over low heat. Leave until the sugar has completely dissolved.

Turn up the heat and simmer until the toffee turns an amber colour.

Remove the pan from the heat and carefully add the lemon juice – take care
as the hot toffee may splutter.

To decorate, quickly dip each apple into the toffee and swirl it around until
evenly coated. Allow to cool for no more than 10 seconds, then dip the
bottoms of the apples in the assorted sprinkles. Sit the apples on baking
parchment to harden. Serve on the same day.

These crunchy morsels are a cinch to make and can be
jiggled around to suit your tastes. For example, if your little
monsters like a double hit of chocolate, add chocolate chips
to the mixture instead of Reese's Pieces. You'll probably
find that adults love these treats as much as the kids do!

brainball clusters

50 g/3 tablespoons butter
50 g/3 tablespoons peanut butter
150 g/5 oz. (about 20) marshmallows
1 tablespoon golden syrup or
light corn syrup
100 g/3 cups crispy rice cereal
75 g/³⁄₄ cup Reese's Pieces or
chocolate chips

TO DECORATE
300 g/10 oz. white chocolate,
chopped
Halloween sprinkles and
sanding sugar

MAKES ABOUT 20

Put the butter, peanut butter, marshmallows and syrup in a small saucepan
over low heat. Stir constantly until the butter and marshmallows have melted
into a smooth, gooey mess.

Pour the crispy rice cereal into a heatproof bowl. Remove the saucepan
from the heat and pour the mixture into the bowl with the cereal. Stir until
thoroughly combined and allow to cool for 3–4 minutes before stirring in the
Reese's Pieces or chocolate chips. Allow to cool until cold.

When completely cold (if you try to do this while the mixture is still warm,
it will stick to your hands in rather an alarming way!), shape the mixture into
large, walnut-size balls between your hands. Place the clusters on a large
sheet of baking parchment.

To decorate, melt the chocolate in a heatproof bowl either in the microwave
on a low setting or over a pan of barely simmering water. Do not let the base
of the bowl touch the water. Stir until smooth.

Using a skewer, spear one brainball cluster at a time and dip into the white
chocolate until evenly coated. Shake off any excess chocolate and place back
on the parchment. Repeat with the remaining clusters and chocolate. Scatter
Halloween sprinkles and/or sanding sugar over them and allow to set.

Surprisingly realistic but very easy to make, these bones can
be made 1–2 days before your Halloween party and stored in an
airtight box. Have fun making them in different shapes and sizes
and giving them away to trick or treaters – that'll scare them!

meringue bones

200 g/1 cup caster/superfine sugar

100 g/3½ oz. egg whites
(from 3–4 eggs)

a pinch of salt

*piping bag, fitted with a plain
1-cm/³⁄₈-inch nozzle/tip*

*2 solid baking sheets, lined with
baking parchment*

MAKES ABOUT 20

Preheat the oven to 200°C (400°F) Gas 6.

Tip the sugar into a small roasting tray and heat on the middle shelf of the preheated oven for about 4 minutes or until hot to the touch.

When the sugar is hot enough, remove from the oven and turn the oven temperature down to 110°C (225°F) Gas ¼.

Put the egg whites and salt in a bowl and whisk with an electric whisk until foamy. Quickly tip all the hot sugar into the bowl and whisk on medium-high speed for about 6 minutes until the meringue is very thick, super glossy and white.

Spoon the meringue into the piping bag. Pipe log shapes, each about 10 cm/4 inches long the baking sheets, spacing them well apart. Pipe 2 balls of meringue at each end of the logs to make a bone shape.

Bake on the middle shelf of the oven for about 40 minutes or until crisp. Turn the oven off and leave the bones to cool inside.

index